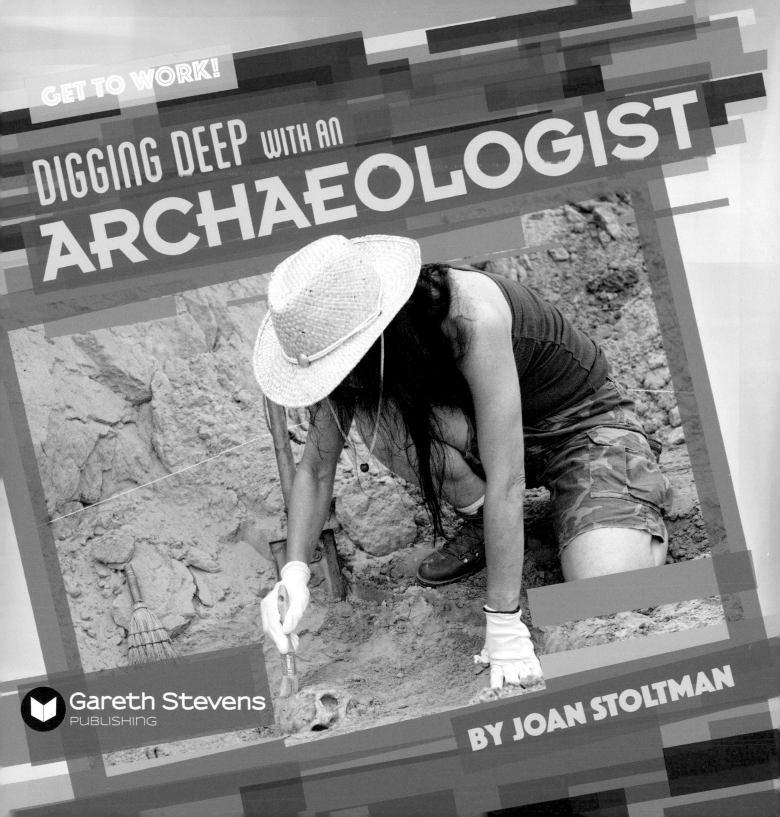

GET TO WORK!

DIGGING DEEP WITH AN ARCHAEOLOGIST

Gareth Stevens
PUBLISHING

BY JOAN STOLTMAN

Please visit our website, www.garethstevens.com. For a free color catalog of all our high-quality books, call toll free 1-800-542-2595 or fax 1-877-542-2596.

Cataloging-in-Publication Data

Names: Stoltman, Joan.
Title: Digging deep with an archaeologist / Joan Stoltman.
Description: New York : Gareth Stevens Publishing, 2019. | Series: Get to work! | Includes index.
Identifiers: ISBN 9781538212264 (pbk.) | ISBN 9781538212271 (library bound) | ISBN 9781538215784 (6 pack)
Subjects: LCSH: Archaeologists–Juvenile literature. | Archaeology–Juvenile literature.
Classification: LCC CC107.S7585 2019 | DDC 930.1–dc23

Published in 2019 by
Gareth Stevens Publishing
111 East 14th Street, Suite 349
New York, NY 10003

Copyright © 2019 Gareth Stevens Publishing

Designer: Bethany Perl
Editor: Joan Stoltman

Photo credits: Cover, p. 1 Microgen/Shutterstock.com; pp. 1-24 (background) MaLija/Shutterstock.com; pp. 1-24 (rectangular banner) punsayaporn/Shutterstock.com; p. 5 Boibin/Shutterstock.com; p. 7 (ancient writing) Fat Jackey/Shutterstock.com; p. 7 (coins) Bukhta Yurii/Shutterstock.com; pp. 8-18 (text box) LoveVectorGirl/Shutterstock.com; p. 9 Igor Matic/Shutterstock.com; p. 11 Gordon Wiltsie/ National Geographic Magazines/Getty Images; pp. 13 (sieve), 19 (scuba divers) Jonathan Blair/ Corbis Documentary/Getty Images; p. 13 (archaeologists) Patricia Hofmeester/Shutterstock.com; p. 14 SAFIN HAMED/AFP/Getty Images p. 15 Richard T. Nowitz/Corbis Documentary/Getty Images; p. 17 SIA KAMBOU/AFP/Getty Images; p. 18 KHALED DESOUKI/AFP/Getty Images; p. 20 Trazos sobre Papel/Shutterstock.com; p. 21 (broken plates) Lestertair/Shutterstock.com; p. 21 (torn paper and tape) Flas100/Shutterstock.com; p. 21 (sand) Walking-onstreet/Shutterstock.com.

CPSIA compliance information: Batch #CS18GS: For further information contact Gareth Stevens, New York, New York at 1-800-542-2595.

CONTENTS

Words in the glossary appear in **bold** type the first time they are used in the text.

WHAT IS ARCHAEOLOGY?

Do you like to dig in the dirt? Are you good at finding things that are lost? Do you love learning about history? Are you a master at **puzzles**? If so, archaeology (ahr-kee-AH-luh-jee) might be for you!

Archaeology is the study of the past through what people have made, used, and left behind. Archaeologists leave rocks and dinosaurs to other scientists and instead study things made by people. The objects archaeologists study are called artifacts. They're found by digging where people have lived.

Archaeologists want to know how people lived, cooked, ate, slept, and more! They also want to learn about rulers, art, beliefs, tools, inventions, and **technology**. They might find bones, but will give them to other scientists to study.

WHAT DO PEOPLE LEAVE BEHIND?

Writing is only about 5,000 years old. That means 99 percent of the past happened without anyone making a record of it! Archaeologists collect and study artifacts to figure out the parts of the past that aren't written down anywhere. Each artifact is like a piece of a larger puzzle.

People leave behind many traces of how they lived. They leave behind tools, buildings, and, best of all, **garbage**! Archaeologists love ancient garbage because it provides clues about what everyday life was like for regular people.

MAKE A COIN!

Create a coin by using a cup to trace a circle on white paper. Write the date and name of where it was made. Now list some ideas of pictures and sayings. Imagine who might discover it in the future. Don't forget to draw on the back!

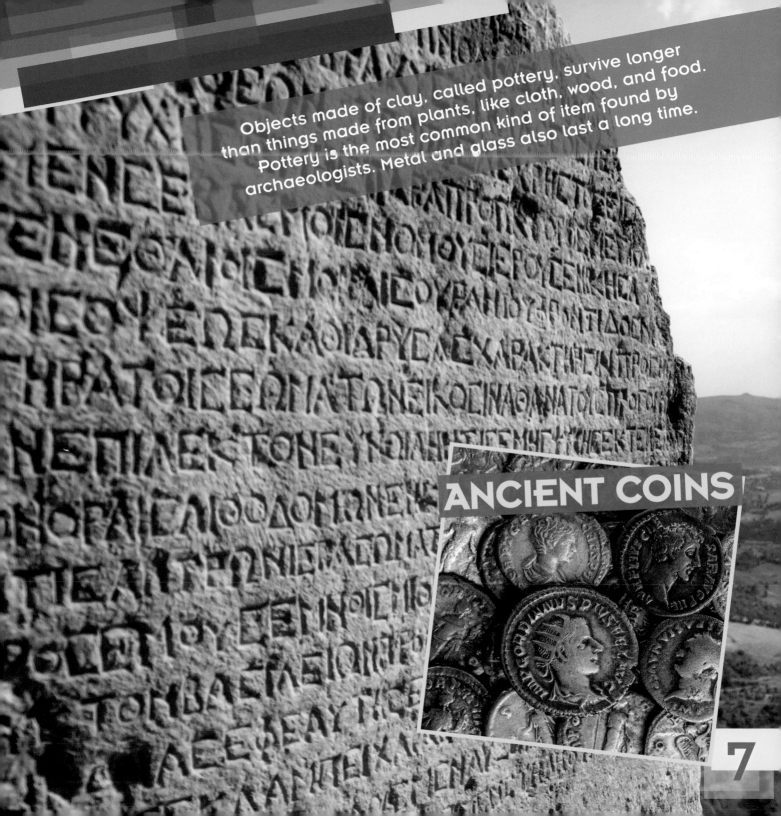

Objects made of clay, called pottery, survive longer than things made from plants, like cloth, wood, and food. Pottery is the most common kind of item found by archaeologists. Metal and glass also last a long time.

ANCIENT COINS

WHERE, OH, WHERE?

It's not easy finding ancient cities under dirt, rocks, and newer buildings. Digging, called excavation, takes a lot of money and time. Archaeologists do lots of **research** about where water, food, and trade routes were to figure out where ancient people lived. They also use new technologies to see underground, underwater, or even through thick forest!

Even with great research, an archaeologist can't just dig anywhere they want. They need to speak to the landowner and sometimes the local government first.

MAKE A MAP!

Archaeologists map the entire site, or place where they're digging, and each part of a site. Practice this skill by mapping your bedroom. Draw as if you were a bird looking down. Be sure to draw windows, doors, and furniture. Label everything!

Sometimes archaeology sites are discovered by chance when gardening, tearing down an old building, or digging for a new home. Someone call an archaeologist!

ON SITE

Imagine you've found a great place to dig, filled with coins, stone walls, and broken pottery. The first thing your team must do is make a **grid** over the excavation site using string and long metal nails.

Then the excavation can begin! You'll soon be surrounded by archaeologists, other scientists, and helpers. They'll carefully dig, brush, **photograph**, and wash each artifact. Don't forget, someone will need to write field notes. This includes labeling, drawing, and adding the artifact's location to the site's map!

EXCAVATE AT HOME!

1. Fill a bucket with a little water.
2. Add a few small toys.
3. **Freeze**.
4. **Repeat** steps 1 through 3 until the bucket is full. Then bring the bucket outside and practice excavating! Ask before using a sharp tool.

The grid is used to keep track of where each artifact is found. Artifacts are labeled on site with their exact location in the grid.

DIGGIN' IT

It's very important to dig slowly and carefully. Remember, you're not just looking for one really cool artifact. The whole site tells a better story than any one artifact from the site.

When a site is excavated, it's destroyed. No one can ever dig that site again! This makes the collection of artifacts very important. It's also why archaeologists write and photograph so much on site. Sometimes, they even leave part of a site alone so future archaeologists with better tools can dig there later.

PRACTICE FIELD NOTES

Borrow three objects from a friend. Take a close look. Write down everything you see. Measure them. Draw their front and back. Who made them? What do they do? Where and when were they made? Who would own them? Write your thoughts.

SIEVE

Brushes, **sieves**, small picks, brooms, and other tools help archaeologists carefully find artifacts in the dirt or sand.

TO THE LAB!

You might think archaeologists spend all their time digging. But for every 1 hour excavating, there can be over 20 hours of **laboratory** work! Each artifact must now get a much closer look. Artifacts are studied in groups based on where they were found in the site's grid.

Finding out the period of time when the site was occupied happens in the lab. If coins with dates on them aren't found, there are several special technologies used to figure out age.

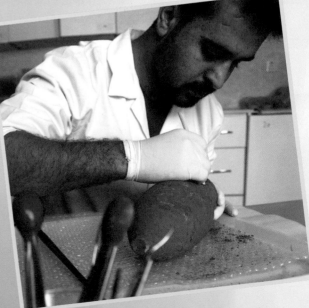

Crossmending means putting broken pieces of pottery together to return it to its original shape. After being photographed, some pottery is taken apart again to be stored in pieces.

15

NOW THE WORK BEGINS!

Cataloging means **describing** something in a planned way, and it's the hardest part of archaeology lab work. Many artifacts will look much like each other, but you'll need to look closely and describe even the tiniest differences. A catalog number is given to each artifact based on where it was found and what else it goes with. All notes, drawings, and photographs are entered into computers. Then each piece is safely stored away in a museum.

This system makes it possible for archaeologists to study the artifacts for years to come.

HEAD TO THE MUSEUM

Visit your local museum to see what's been discovered in your area!

Researching an entire site—and all its artifacts—can take years. When an archaeologist has a new idea about how people may have lived, they'll write a book or article to share it with the world!

WHAT IT TAKES

As you might have guessed, archaeologists need a lot of different kinds of knowledge and skills. They use math, history, art history, and many kinds of science every day!

You'll have to do a lot of training after high school. In **college**, and in school after college, you'll help on a lot of digs! During college, you can choose what you want to know more about, like a certain kind of artifact, time period, people, or place.

RECOVERING A STATUE

Underwater archaeologists work with special technology to excavate sites that are underwater! Zooarchaeologists (zoh-ahr-kee-AH-luh-jists) study animal remains from sites to see what people ate, how they hunted, and how they raised animals.

19

A FUTURE ARCHAEOLOGIST?

So much of what's happened on Earth is still unknown. Maybe you'll be the one to figure out why and how Stonehenge was built! Or maybe you'll discover things that help the world with the illnesses and food problems of today! You may even prove an idea we've believed for a long time is wrong.

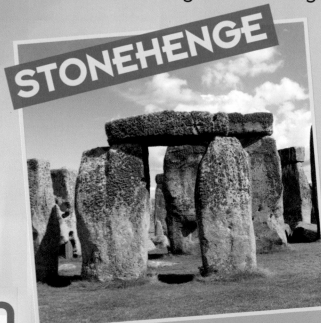

STONEHENGE

If you're good at working on a team, love science, enjoy history, and are willing to spend years solving a puzzle, then archaeology is just the field for you!

Archaeologists spend a lot of time putting pottery back together. It's never the same twice! Make sure you're with an adult for this project.

PUT IT BACK TOGETHER

YOU'LL NEED

cheap pottery dishes with patterns

a box

dirt or sand

tape

plastic bag that closes

tweezers

fork

LEVEL 1

1. Have an adult break one dish inside a closed bag.
2. With an adult, bury the pieces in a box of dirt or sand.
3. Using a fork and tweezers, carefully find each piece. Set them aside.
4. Put the pieces back together using tape.

LEVEL 2

As an archaeologist, you won't know what an artifact looked like before it was broken. So without you seeing the dish's shape or pattern, repeat steps 1-4.

LEVEL 3

While excavating, you'll often have pieces from more than one broken artifact found near each other. So using two dishes instead of one, repeat steps 1-4.

LEVEL 4

At a site, some pieces may never be found. So repeat steps 1-4, but leave out 4 of the broken pieces.

GLOSSARY

college: a school after high school

describe: to say what something or someone is like

freeze: to become a solid, such as ice, because of cold

garbage: things that are no longer useful or wanted and that have been thrown out

grid: a set of squares formed by crisscrossing lines

laboratory: a place with tools to perform experiments

photograph: to take a picture of someone or something by using a camera, or the picture made by a camera

puzzle: a question or problem that requires thought, skill, or cleverness to be answered or solved

repeat: to make, do, or say something again

research: studying to find something new

sieve: a tool used to separate large bits of matter from smaller bits of matter

technology: the way people do something using tools and the tools they use

FOR MORE INFORMATION

Books

Hartland, Jessie. *How the Flag Got to the Museum.* Maplewood, NJ: Blue Apple Books, 2015.

Hartland, Jessie. *How the Sphinx Got to the Museum.* Maplewood, NJ: Blue Apple Books, 2010.

Logan, Claudia. *The 5,000-Year-Old Puzzle: Solving a Mystery of Ancient Egypt.* New York, NY: Farrar Straus Giroux, 2002.

Websites

A Kid's Guide to Archaeology on the Coconino National Forest
www.fs.usda.gov/Internet/FSE_DOCUMENTS/stelprdb5360668.pdf
You can read or print and color this neat booklet on archaeology!

Arctic Artifacts
www.nps.gov/webrangers/activities/artifact/?id=02
Click through this online activity to learn what an archaeologist does at a site.

Tools of the Trade
amnh.org/explore/ology/archaeology/tools-of-the-trade2
Play this online game to learn all about an archaeologist's tools.

INDEX